Portraits of Faith and Freedom

Portraits of Faith and Freedom
Copyright © 2022 by Linda L. Blum

Published in the United States of America

ISBN Paperback: 978-1-959165-27-9
ISBN eBook: 978-1-959165-28-6

All rights reserved. No part of this publication may be reproduced, stored in a retrieval system or transmitted in any way by any means, electronic, mechanical, photocopy, recording or otherwise without the prior permission of the author except as provided by USA copyright law.

ReadersMagnet, LLC
10620 Treena Street, Suite 230 | San Diego, California, 92131 USA
1.619. 354. 2643 | www.readersmagnet.com

Book design copyright © 2022 by ReadersMagnet, LLC. All rights reserved.
Cover design by Kent Gabutin
Interior design by Dorothy Lee

Portraits
of Faith and Freedom

LINDA L. BLUM

ReadersMagnet, LLC

DEDICATION

To my siblings,

Although you live far from me, you are always close to my heart.

INTRODUCTION

"I was lonely until I got a best friend. Even now, I miss her, my Henny-Penny. My pet hen followed me everywhere." This is a quote from one of the stories in *Portraits of Faith and Freedom*.

The portraits of the people in this book will inspire you to believe that you too can overcome challenges in your own life. These are true stories from people I know personally; they aren't autobiographies, rather, they are memoirs of an important aspect of their lives they have shared with me during interviews.

I cherish the trust these dear ones have placed in me and have endeavored to write their stories graciously and discreetly. Some of them have chosen to change their names, locations, and identifying information of peripheral people. I hold the utmost honor and appreciation for each one who shared his/her heart for this book.

The book has Parts one and two; Part one is a compilation of sixteen life-stories, and Part two consists of my responses to four main themes derived from the stories. After a lifetime of experience helping people of all ages, I shared some things I've learned in Part Two.

Note: The beautiful color portrait, used by permission, is of Sonja Stefan from her story "All Things Made New."

CHAPTERS

Dedication iv
Introduction v

PART ONE

Blessed With Shalom 1
Never Turn Back 5
Lamb Among Wolves 15
Healed: Body, Soul, And Spirit 21
Forty-Year Prayer Answered 26
America In My Heart 29
A Light To Follow 32
When He Became Lord 35
Beyond The Expected 37
All Things Made New 40
A Party Brought Hope 43
Light From Darkness 46
Heavenly Rescue 49
From Fear To Faith 52
All For His Glory 56
But For Grace 60

PART TWO

Training Children 64
Inspiring Youth 67
Supporting Women 70
Understanding The New Age 73

BLESSED WITH SHALOM

Leah

10,000 Reasons

*"Bless the LORD, O my soul, O my soul;
worship His holy name..."
(Matt Redman, England, 2011)*

"Your mother asked me to bring you back." The man towered over me as he leaned against the car.

"You're a stranger, and I'm not supposed to talk to you!" I rose up menacingly.

"I'm a policeman." The man grinned and gently touched my shoulder. "Your mother described you to me. Isn't your name Leah?" I slowly nodded.

"Come on, Get in." I eagerly plunked on the car seat. For a three year-old, riding in a police car was a big adventure. Earlier, I had left the department store and crossed two busy city streets. The policeman found me in the park playing with pigeons.

I bless the Lord for all He has done for me during all of my life's adventures, misadventures, joys, sorrows, and victories.

I was welcomed into the world in 1947 at the Eastern Hospital in New Jersey, the first child of Jewish parents. Two years later a brother was born.

My father was living in New Jersey when my mother was hired to work in his law firm. She and her father had been allowed to leave their home in Hitler's Germany to move to Switzerland because her father had been born there. After a short time in that country, they immigrated to America.

My paternal grandparents and my maternal grandfather lived in New Jersey. I still remember going on walks with my sweet grandmother. "Walking with you is like walking with a cute puppy dog." She pulled me to her side, and we walked that way. I felt warm inside.

Our family traveled to Europe often for vacations. I remember England, Ireland, Holland, Switzerland, Germany, and France. One incident from my childhood causes me to giggle when I think about it. We were staying in a hotel in London when I was ten. My parents had hired a babysitter because they were going to Dad's client's home for dinner. I had an intestinal problem so my mother called. "We need to cancel dinner tonight. We're not comfortable leaving our daughter with a babysitter."

"Please bring your children." We were late getting there because of taking a subway to the wrong neighborhood. All the people we approached for help spoke either Spanish or Italian. Finally, a taxi brought us to a fancy house where we were made welcome. A rotund butler, his tux jacket buttons about to pop, met us and led us to an ornate dining room.

Wine was served to all of us by the smiling butler. He kept filling my glass with wine. "Please, Leah has had enough." My mother was getting concerned when I started giggling.

"Oh, but this is Europe," he smiled at me while he filled my glass to the brim. "Drink up, Girl." His voice sounded far away. I was a little bit drunk!

My childhood home life was happy with my parents and brother until one terrible day in early June when I was twelve. Dad was late coming home from work. "I wonder what's keeping him." Mom had a "worry" face. Zing! Zing! Mom hurried to answer the doorbell and found two policemen outside our door.

"There's been an accident, Ma'am. We're sorry to tell you that your husband didn't make it." *From this day on our lives will never be the same.* I ran to my mother.

I was to play my viola for the first time in the middle school orchestra on the same day as the funeral. The funeral was in the morning, and the music event was in the evening. My school exerted no pressure, but my mother decided that I should play. "We have to go on with our lives," she said with a sad smile.

Looking back, I think that's what my father would have wanted. Oh, how I missed him! We had enjoyed playing chess often, and I missed having fun with Dad.

Music became my passion; I was second soprano in the school chorus, and the viola became my favorite instrument. I was fortunate to have excellent music teachers for singing, piano, and viola. I also played the accordion and the violin.

While teaching music at a day camp when I was a teenager, I discovered that teaching music was the career path for me. My mother was a teacher, and I admired the teachers I had at school.

I have always been socially awkward, so I was an easy target for bullies. Bullying was relentless during my elementary and middle school years. One day in my fourth-grade classroom I yanked out a bully's chair when she was getting ready to sit; my teacher was delighted that I had finally taken a step to fight back.

I received an MS degree in Music Ed. While student teaching, I realized I wanted to concentrate on strings. In addition, I have taught singing and helped direct musicals. I also studied Music Therapy for people with special needs which included an internship. I have taught hundreds of students since then, some becoming professional.

Even though I enjoyed my work, there was a deep void in my life. It seemed to be a spiritual lack. My family celebrated the major holidays of Judaism, and I attended Religious School as a Jewish child. However, when I was twelve I didn't have a Bat Mitzvah; rather, I was confirmed at fifteen.

All my life my precious Mom has been a constant support and guide. She taught me what I needed to know in order to be successful in the practical aspects of my life. I loved to cook, and she gave me a box of handwritten recipes. I was by her side when she passed. I was relieved that she was no longer suffering, but the grief was unbearable.

Shortly afterward, a Christian friend encouraged me to attend a church service one Sunday morning. After the service that had answered a lot of questions, several wonderful people helped me discover Yeshua Ha Mashiach (Jesus the Messiah.) He filled the void in my life with joy, peace, and hope for my future. Interestingly, I found that many of my Jewish ancestors had held a belief in Yeshua, including some who had written books. Because of my faith in Yeshua, I am very aware of the presence of God. He is most real to me when I'm outside enjoying nature.

My parting words are: God has always led me in the right way and His provision for my needs has never run out. The most important focus of my life is: "But seek first the kingdom of God and His righteousness, and all these things shall be added to you." (Matthew 6:33 NKJV)

NEVER TURN BACK

Susan

How Firm a Foundation

*"How firm a foundation, ye saints of the Lord is
laid for your faith in His excellent Word..."
(John Rippon, England, 1787)*

Have you ever argued with God? Well, I did when I heard in my spirit His unmistakable voice. "Help that man." Oh, I knew He meant the town drunk. "That man" lived in his car even when the temperature fell to -40oF. Later, he lived in a small camper at the pond near my house. "No Lord, that's the town drunk!" I wondered too if I had heard right. To be honest, I was afraid of him. "I died for him too. Change your attitude, daughter."

The first time I met "that man" I was with a couple, Mike and Martha, I had met that day. We were at the pond where I taught kids to swim. The town drunk came over to us. "My name is Gary. I bet you can't teach me to swim." He was challenging me.

"I can teach anybody to swim. But you have to put your beer down; take off your boots, and get in the water."

Mike interrupted us, "Give me a chance to run home to get you a pair of shorts." He returned with them, and then Gary had his first swimming lesson. I didn't know then how much I'd learn from him.

I made my appearance in 1947 at Schenectady, New York in the Union Hospital. My parents and my older brother welcomed me. Our family grew when two younger sisters were born. My brother and I felt we were wanted, but it became clear that the younger ones didn't enjoy that status.

My father was an atheist, but my mother brought us to church. When I was five years old, I cried during a sermon. My mother said, "You're crazy to cry in church." To her, going to church was a social duty. I loved Jesus and often sang the song: *I Believe* when I was five.

At fifteen I became pregnant. My seventeen year-old boyfriend married me before my son was born. My mother made me wear a red dress for the wedding. My husband and I moved into a cottage behind my in-laws' home. On my mother's birthday six weeks before I became sixteen my son was born. "I don't want to hold him." Mom was stubborn and emphatic folding her arms as she stood stiffly in my hospital room.

A nurse frowned and said, "Ma'am, hold your grandson."

My mother took him, but maintained a nasty look and didn't even look at his face. I read the "Bastard Child" look on her face

Our little family went home to the cottage; the grandparents were elated when they met their grandson. They treated me with kindness and taught me how to be a mother. On the other hand, my scowling parents said, "Finish high school, or we will disown you." Later, when my son and I visited, my father sternly said, "Go away. You're bad." I was devastated to leave my siblings, only three and five years old at that time. I rarely saw them after that day.

I delivered a daughter when I was seventeen. I felt that I was a good mother, and took good care of my children for seven years. I had given up spending time with my high school friends; I lived my life for my children.

I knew others were becoming hippies and taking LSD. Timothy Leary, the leader of the hippie movement, was convincing when he declared, "Turn on. Tune in. Drop out. Everyone who wants to be happy in life and to find God should follow that." After I had been a responsible parent for seven years, I wanted to do what Leary promoted.

My husband told me I couldn't come back if I left, and he and his parents cared for our children. Then, my new boyfriend and I hitch hiked to California to join the hippies. We took LSD, and I had hallucinations that were red, white, and blue cloud formations spelling Pepsi Cola. I knew I was far gone, but I didn't believe Pepsi Cola was God!

I had two abortions and gave birth to two sons, and my husband and I got divorced. My boyfriend and I moved to Maine where he married me giving his name to our two boys so he could get custody of them when we divorced. Again, I wore a red dress. *Bad girl…*

I worked at a church vestment factory. I liked working there on the line, but I wanted to make hand-embroidered items. I made hand-embroidered shirts at home and sold them in the breakroom. A Christian coworker gave me rides to work. He shared the truth of the gospel as I held a small New Testament that had been given to my oldest son.

Before work one morning, I knelt in front of the woodstove. "Lord, my life is a mess. I confess that I've had two abortions…" I cried out to God confessing and asking forgiveness as I recalled how I'd messed up my life. "I believe you, Jesus; I know that you paid for my sins. Please help me be a good mother for my two little boys."

That same day my boss sauntered into the breakroom. "I see you do hand-embroidery. The lady who does it is going blind, so she's quit. Will you do it for us?"

"Yes, but may I do it at home?" I was smiling so much my cheeks tingled. The desire of my heart was to stay at home to raise my boys. I had hand-embroidered butterflies I mounted in frames to sell, but that hadn't worked out. The Lord gave me the desire of my heart when my boss said I could work from home. All of that happened just two hours after I had prayed! Psalm 37:4 says: "Delight yourself also in the Lord, and He shall give you the desires of your heart."

Since that day, I have never turned back to my old ways. I found a good church nearby and served in the children's department for many years. Also, once each month I ministered in a nursing home. The activities director told me the residents liked to sing. "Do you know how to play the piano?"

I answered, "Yes, I do."

After the people were brought into the room, the director gestured toward me. "We have a pianist with us." I sat at the piano and led them in familiar hymns. Gradually I related with the residents as I returned regularly playing and singing.

Another day the director asked if anyone knew how to make quilts. Being a quilt maker, I volunteered. I made the squares and taught the ladies how to sew them together. While they sewed they opened up about their lives. One special lady, Helen, told how her mother had died. Her mother's friend had typhoid fever, and she went to her friend's home to help her in spite of her husband's objections. Helen told me that her mother had died from typhoid fever and that afterward she had assumed the responsibility of raising her siblings. I sent up a quick prayer and told her, "Jesus said no greater love has one but to lay down his life for a friend." She was finally comforted when she understood the love her mother had shown.

On days that I worked substituting in housekeeping and laundry, I walked up and down the halls playing my banjo during my breaks.. I played and sang songs from the WWI era. "Until we Meet Again" was a favorite. Gaining permission from the head nurse to sing for a dying patient, I stepped over to Helen's bedside with my banjo. *Just over in the Glory Land* was the song I chose to play and sing. As the last note faded out, Helen went to Heaven.

I went to college and acquired a degree for Occupational Therapy Assistant. I became certified and worked as a COTA for seventeen years. During that time I bought a small house. My husband was unbearably mean during our marriage, and I knew I couldn't get a divorce until after both boys had graduated from high school. After they graduated, we were divorced, and I moved into the little house.

Doors opened for me to join a band, the Good News Gospel Team, playing the banjo and singing. I met many quadriplegic people; in fact, every Sunday afternoon we rehearsed in the living room of a dear quad couple. The band played once a month in seven nursing homes for seven years. When many of the members became disabled, we stopped playing together.

I dreamed of the day when I'd own property at the pond where I swam with my boys. However, I was afraid of the scary town drunk who lived in his car on the pond property. The police forced him to get out. His brother let him come on his property, but he kept going back to the pond where the police kicked him out again and again.

In the introductory part of my story I told of teaching Gary to swim. I arrived for the second lesson and noticed he was sitting in his car fully dressed. "How long will it take you to get ready for your lesson?"

"I don't need another lesson." He folded his arms.

I looked in the window. "I've passed by you for years. Would you be willing to tell me your story?"

" I'm a dying alcoholic. I have six months to live. I'm going to drink myself to death and go to Hell."

Hiding my shock I asked, "Are you happy with your life?"

"No. I hate it."

"I know Jesus; He's no respecter of persons. I belonged to a band. Our guitarist was in the same hole as you. Jesus brought him out of it, and He will do the same for you."

He gripped both sides of the steering wheel. "I'm in the middle of these two guys."

"Who are the guys?"

"Satan is on one side. God is on the other, and I am in the middle"

"Listen, God *won't* make you do anything, and Satan *can't* make you do anything. It is your choice whom you will follow. I work a full time job, but I'm inviting you to come to my house in the evenings for six weeks. You'll learn about the Lord by hanging out with a Christian."

I'll never forget the first time he drove up my driveway. He wanted to hide his car behind the house. "I don't want people to see the town drunk going to see the holy woman."

"Leave the car in the driveway and come in." I opened the door, and Gary shuffled in.

I sat at the piano. "Do you know Elvis Presley sings Gospel songs? Do you have a favorite one?" I asked.

"I know Elvis sings Gospel songs." He settled in a rocking chair ready to listen.

I played and sang many older hymns, such as *What a Friend, Amazing Grace, and In the Garden*. I noticed his eyes brimming with tears.

"I'm not crying; something is bothering my eyes. I need to go now, but I'll be back." True to his word, he came for six weeks. I began to realize how God had prepared me all those years to meet all of the challenges I would face. What surprises God had in store!

Gary went with me when I bought four acres of the lakeside property. Soon after, I took my disabled friend Cynthia to see the property. She was excited when she saw the potential there. "You could turn this into a wheelchair woods." Gary, standing with us, thought hers was a great idea.

Gary was eager to help me having the skills necessary to accomplish the daunting task of clearing the land. Soon we were making trails; Gary, a woodcutter knew how to trim the trees to make it a beautiful place. He knew what needed to be done. Soon, there were brush piles and felled trees.

He came up with another idea. "We could make a dock so people in wheelchairs can fish." Next, that sturdy, accessible dock was built by him by my friends and I.

The police had kicked Gary off the property, and his trailer was at his brother's place. I asked him to move his trailer back to my property to act as caretaker.

"I can't do that. The police will kick me out again." Gary shook his head.

I put up a sign by his camper: "*GARY HAND CARETAKER: What he says goes.*" Sure enough the police came to kick him out again, but he spoke to them as he pointed at the sign, "What I say goes. You have to go. I stay."

People came to enjoy outdoor activities, many of them for the first time in decades. However, Gary was still drinking. The evidence was the 55 gal. barrel that was full of beer cans every two weeks. *Lord. Someday these will be soda cans.*

One day I told Gary, "I am going to climb Bigelow Mountain."

"I'll come to protect you."

"OK, but I think it's better if you climb White Cap first and then be able to walk the next day. You can't drink beer and climb a mountain. I'll bring water, sandwiches, peanut butter cheese crackers, and peanut M&Ms."

On the day of the hike, he announced, "I'm not thirsty or hungry." We had been climbing for a while when he collapsed on the trail. "I can't do it." Gary was weak.

I offered some food but ended up force-feeding the peanut M&Ms. Then, he drank water and ate some crackers that revived and strengthened him..

We hiked to the top where the 360o view was breathtaking. I pulled out my Bible and read the parable of the rich man and Lazarus. (I thought my reading that passage on the mountaintop was strange, but years later I learned that his father had died shortly before. Was his dad warning, "Don't come here, son.") We hiked back down, but Gary was shaking. He had never gone a whole day without booze. We stopped at a store and bought a beer.

Over the years, Gary was in the hospital at death's door many times. I worked nearby, so I went to be with him on my lunch hour. The nurses thought I was his girlfriend. I told them I was just trying to show him a better life. Once, the doctor told me, "He'll be dead soon." I asked my pastor to pray that he'd go home to die. She said she'd pray that he'd go home to live.

Lord, is there anything else I can do? At that particular time Gary had been in a coma for weeks. An answer came immediately, "Daughter, he'll wake up when you play and sing his favorites. I brought my keyboard and played his most favorite: *When the Angels Rejoice*. When I left he was still comatose. However, the next day his nurse came running up to me, "Go in and see!" Gary was sitting up and grinning when I entered.

"Where were you? You were gone a long time."

"I went up in the sky to a big gate and the gatekeeper told me, "It's not your time. You have to go back." I knew then that he'd made his peace with God. That week he was transferred to the nursing home where I worked.

After he went back to his trailer, I realized he was no longer drinking (never again). He asked if he could live in the space above my garage. I replied, "We can build an apartment there for you." Before he moved, I put Bible story pictures and scriptures on the newly insulated walls and tarp ceiling. Gary was happy to live in a nice place and enjoyed gazing at the pictures and verses, especially when ill.

For sixteen wonderful years, Gary and I worked together blessing many groups of physically challenged people. The recreation area upkeep was a lot of hard work, but there was always joy and laughter.

After two strokes and residual paralysis, Gary continued to have a zest for life and began attending church. He was a blessing to everyone he met. That alcoholism was miraculously gone for good. I had obeyed the Lord and fulfilled His mission. He had blessed me with an unexpected, wonderful friendship.

The Lord called me for another mission. I was to begin a sewing school in Uganda, Africa. Through fundraising efforts, I raised enough money from local churches to buy six treadle sewing machines and supplies. In Uganda I started a sewing school to teach girls and women how to make clothing, especially uniforms. While I was there five times, I also taught songs to the school children.

Although the doctors said Gary would never walk again, he proved them wrong. He did walk and shared how God had changed his life with everyone who came to the pond. The man who had scared me became my friend and a friend of Jesus. Gary Hand, the Miracle Man, has now been enjoying his heavenly home ever since Christmas Eve, 2016.

Shortly before he died, we were watching *The Life of Billy Graham* when Gary exclaimed, "I recognize him. I always liked watching him on television." *That was before I met him...*

Hmmm, the town drunk watched Billy Graham!!!! Billy Graham had planted the seed; I was honored to harvest his soul.

Dear reader, my story shows the miracle-working power and love of God for you just as you are. "For as the heavens are higher than the earth, so are my ways higher than your ways."
(Isaiah 55:9 NKJV)

LAMB AMONG WOLVES

Lucy

I Will Glory in My Redeemer

*"I will glory in my redeemer,
whose priceless blood has ransomed me..."
(Steve and Vicki Cook, USA, 2000)*

What can this mother do? My husband couldn't come with my son and me on the day of Chris' testing. Holding the hand of our four year-old son I pushed the door open. Behind a large oak desk sat the neuropsychologist. He wore a black, red, and white checked bowtie, and he had a long face with a pointy nose that balanced his wire-rimmed glasses. "Ma'am, I'm going to read your son's diagnosis now." He cleared his throat as he reached for the folder. "Significant Neurological- Language Disorder impacting reading and writing, speaking, poor fine and gross motor skills, expressive and receptive processing deficits, executive functioning disorder, and short term memory weaknesses. This requires placement in substantially separate special education schools and programs." He closed the folder and looked me square in the eyes. "Get prepared, Ma'am." I was in shock frozen to the chair.

I felt a headache coming on. "What does all that mean?"

"Your son will struggle with expressing himself and understanding others, problem-solving, and feeling comfortable in the world around him. All academics and hands-on activities will be a major challenge for the boy." I glanced at Chris playing in the corner.

When Chris was six, he was tested again. The good news was that he tested in the genius range with visual detail. The doctor said, "The real challenge is that he will understand what is normal, but he won't be able to achieve it. His childhood will be Hell." Tested at eight, he was further diagnosed as having severe anxiety, mild depression, ADHD, and OCD. Meds were ordered to help control the symptoms.

What will this mother do? She will support the boy she loves and will PRAY. My story will highlight the spiritual journey my son and I walked together.

PRAYER CHANGED EVERYTHING

I was born in Delaware, the only girl among three brothers, two older and one younger. Feelings of rejection and insecurity plagued my childhood. I felt unimportant and neglected.

My family lived in the country, next door to over twenty relatives. I was close to my cousins; one of them, when we were adults, challenged me to pray and was instrumental in my coming to faith. Through prayer I was able to overcome my insecurities and became a happier mother and wife.

My husband and I had three children. My story is centered on my middle child, Chris. From kindergarten through twelfth grade he attended seven different schools. I still hear the echo of Chris's plaintive cry. "Why are we looking at this school? I don't belong here. When we had the tour, I saw a girl eating her hair."

I wept for my son, but suddenly I felt the Lord's presence. *I love him more than you ever possibly can. I've got him. I won't let him go.* Like Hannah in the Bible, I gave my son completely to God. The LORD comforted my heart that day, but Chris and I were on a rollercoaster ride and would witness volcanic eruptions for many years.

When Chris turned thirteen, we decided to bring him to a residential school. I had prayed and felt it was God's will. I'll never forget that heart wrenching day when I brought him back from Christmas vacation. He ran after me screaming. "I hate it here! They are so mean! I want to go back home! You don't have to leave me. Bring me home now."

Every atom of my being wanted to fulfill his plea. While driving home a guttural cry erupted from deep inside, and the floodgates opened. All too familiar refrains swirled in my mind. "I am a fool to have thought I knew God's plans; I am to blame for all of my son's misery. My sweet-natured boy is drowning in a pond of fear and insecurity. He thinks his mother has abandoned him. I am killing his innocence, sensitivity, and sweet loving nature. How could I have been so stupid?"

I was listening to the voice of the enemy of my soul and sinking into a greater and greater darkness. I hated myself and felt like a failure. My mind was caught in a quagmire of fear and confusion. As soon as I arrived home, I sped up the driveway, and leapt from my car. I raced to the front door. *Please, please answer.* She answered on the second ring. I poured out all I was feeling, and my friend and prayer partner poured God's love and hope into my confused, distraught, and weary spirit.

I had received God's instructions to pursue an open and honest conversation with the staff and to put my trust in my Savior. I prayed that they'd hear my concerns about Chris' emotional state. Peace filled my heart as I drifted off to sleep with my Bible open at Psalm 91.

By God's grace I was able to speak the truth in love. The austere principal's veneer cracked, and her eyes filled with tears. Afterwards, I sought counsel from our neuropsychologist and was advised to seek yet another placement.

Three schools later, Chris returned home. At this time he was exhibiting severe behavior problems along with incessant worrying. He had meltdowns and panic attacks. After finding him curled up in a closet one day Chris' fifteen-year old brother hugged me. "Don't worry, Mom. I'll take care of him." We learned that Chris had been constantly bullied and unjustly treated by both adults and children. Their actions included: being shoved into lockers, pushed down steep inclines, slapped across the back of his head, and falsely accused a number of times. Lamb among wolves!

Every time a professional said, "Chris may need to live with you even into adulthood. He probably won't go to college and most likely will end up with a menial job," the Lord would speak to my heart. *I have a plan for Chris' life, plans to give him a future full of hope. All things are possible for he who believes.* I discovered that I no longer rode the emotional rollercoaster while putting trust in God more and more each day..

Chris hated his final secondary school, but in God's providence, a compassionate teacher helped him pass the state testing. This enabled him to secure a high school diploma. It was a proud moment for our dear son, and the whole family pitched in to celebrate with a graduation party on our lawn. All the extended family came and showered Chris with gifts, especially what he'd need for his college living quarters.

The next hurdle was college. Chris was determined to go, and despite the severity of his dyslexia he was able to participate in a college LD program with intensive tutorial support. However, his freshman year was cut short due to his escalating anxiety and behaviors

Back home again, he procured a job as a dishwasher. Within a month he erupted like a volcano. He walked through the restaurant ranting, "I wasn't paid!" Storming to the outside he began running down the streets banging on cars.

"Dear Lord, help him to find your plan. Anxiety is a monster!" For the next nine months Chris holed up in our attic playroom watching movies and playing video games. He was imprisoned by anxiety and too afraid to face the world. We received the message that God had a plan "to flip the switch on the crippling fear."

Soon, bored and restless, Chris was ready to confront the world again. We enrolled him in a seven-week film school where he pulled through victoriously. He even was able to came off all his meds at once.

The real breakthrough came after two weeks of being a camp counselor. Chris called home. "I was being teased and bullied. I went to my room and lost it. I just started screaming at the top of my lungs. I exploded like a volcano. Now they're asking me to leave. I want Jesus to heal me. I can't take this anymore." Chris had finally turned to Jesus!

My husband threw in the towel at this point. Chris applied to a Christian Internship program three quarters of the way across the nation. Before we left home to drive there, Chris had an upset stomach. "Mom, I won't let Satan stop me now." We headed west not being entirely sure that Chris had been accepted to the program. In the hotel one morning Chris was taking a shower when he felt dizzy, his vision blurred, and he fell. I brought him out to the bedroom and began to pray for my unconscious son. Shortly he looked up at me. "My mind is calm." God had delivered Chris. The anxiety monster was gone. He had a sound mind.

After He was set free, Chris continued with his schooling and earned a Bachelor of Arts in Film and Photography. He's traveled the world and currently lives independently. Oh, God surely had a hope and a future for Chris. Now he prays as he walks the city streets and shares the love of Jesus with whoever crosses his path.

What is a mother to do? Pray and believe that "with God ALL things are possible." I turned to the LORD of my life, and He did the impossible. "His mercies are new each morning. His compassion never fails, great is His faithfulness." (Lamentations 3:22-23)

HEALED: BODY, SOUL, AND SPIRIT

Albert

Amazing Grace

"Amazing grace, how sweet the sound, that saved a wretch like me…" (John Newton, England, 1779)

Ouch! My stomach hurt from hunger; I bent over to try to get some relief. When I was only twelve, my stepfather violently kicked me out of my home onto the street. Crawling into a dumpster, I pulled out chicken feet and a loaf of greenish-blue bread. I scraped off the mold and ate some of the bread ignoring the foul taste as much as I could. I tried to chew the chicken feet after ripping off the feathers that clung to the top.

My story is all about survival, freedom, and miracles. Even though some parts may seem like "idle tales", every word is the truth; in fact, eye witnesses are still alive and talking about the amazing miracles.

My story begins in Malawi in the North Central region. Dad and Mom were married bringing me up until I was four years old. That was when my father left for the UK and another wife. Being a Christian woman, my mother didn't believe in polygamy so they divorced.

When I was twelve years old, Mom married a man from Malawi. He hated me. "Get out now!" he shouted as he pointed his spear at me. I climbed a tree for overnight shelter sleeping fitfully. During the days that followed, I met people who I asked for work. Some said "No" and some said "Yes." Once in a while people gave me money.

I hung out near a store. One day the manager got my attention. "Would you run some errands for us?"

Immediately, I straightened. "Yes, Sir." I liked working for that kind man, and after a few weeks of being with him, I asked him to be my father.

"Yes, I'll adopt you." He smiled and continued, "You'll become our son." He was married and had two children, a baby and a toddler. His wife gave me a hug in welcome. They were a Christian couple who always showed love toward me.

I had lived with them for a year when Dad was transferred to another franchise. We all moved to the capital city of Lilongave. I was enrolled in school. After only one month, he died in a car accident. After I had lived in their home for another month, Mom approached me, "Please sit. I want to talk with you." She brought a chair close to me. "It makes me very sad, but I have to ask you to leave. I can't afford for you to stay here any longer." Our tears mingled as we hugged.

I was thirteen and on the street again, but the new manager, also a Christian, brought me into his family. "I know all about you, my dear boy, and you are invited to live with us as our son." He was married and had two sons. I was enrolled in school after taking the National Exam. I was skipped two grades and was placed in a higher level school.

When I was seventeen, sad news came that Dad had died that day in a bus accident. Soon, his wife asked me to leave for financial reasons. I wondered," *Am I somehow causing their deaths? Two dads have died in four years!"*

I lived on the street again, and all I cared about was surviving. Meeting other boys who were also homeless, I formed a gang. It was a wild life of violence and substance abuse for six years. At night I had my gang activities, but during the day I attended a distance-learning college. I graduated from the four-year culinary college and worked as head chef at a hotel. While working there, I developed a severe gastric illness losing a lot of weight. I was sick only at work, so I felt I was under a curse from the previous head chef who was mad that I was hired to take his place. My doctor said, "You're going to die." That was when I decided to quit. After I resigned, I wasn't sick anymore. Soon I found a chef job at a local restaurant.

One of the owner's two sons was the head of a gang of thieves, killing and looting. I joined his gang. We went to my father's house to steal from him. Because he had left me, I was angry and got revenge by robbing him. I didn't know until later that he had been saved and was a pastor. He had been praying for me but didn't know where to find me. In fact, when I came with the gang, he didn't recognize me.

The gang leader had a pregnant girlfriend that he beat often. She was bruised when she came to ask for help. I gave her money when she showed me her album, pictures of the beatings. She left their apartment. That evening, my door swung open to reveal the red-faced drunk boyfriend. "YOU...YOU!" He stumbled into my apartment and spotted the photo album his girlfriend had left. He beat me severely and stumbled out.

I was ready to go unconscious, but I murmured my desperation. "God, help me!"

Waking up in the hospital near death with bandages and tubes all over my body, I was startled to see that an angel appeared by my bedside. "Albert, you've been healed. God is calling you to go on the streets to minister to the street kids. They are God's children." *I am saved, healed, and called all at the same time!*

My nurse came toward my bed. "What???" I thought she might faint when she saw the tubes had popped out leaving no holes and her patient was totally healed standing beside the bed. After I explained what had happened, she prayed and was saved.

All seven patients on the ward were saved and healed, and we all left the hospital. My nurse is still telling all that happened that day. Two of the patients are ministers.

I went from the hospital to a church. After I spent some time with the pastor, he offered that I could live at the church. I went to my apartment to gather my belongings but discovered that it was completely empty. All I had were the bloody clothes I was wearing. The pastor's son gave me a shirt and pants.

Every day I read the Bible and prayed, cleaned the church, tended gardens, and prayed with people. I started a small group and went on the street to help the kids. I wanted to attend a Bible college even though I had no money, outfits, or personal hygiene products.

One day after spending time praying on a mountain, I received an anonymous letter. All my needs were met, even spending money, until I graduated.

After graduating, I met a woman from the United States who was in Malawi for a short-term mission. I was surprised when she told me about her call. "The LORD called me to minister to the street kids." We married, and for five years we ministered to the Malawi street kids. Now we are enjoying our life with our two kids, a boy and a girl. We are youth pastors in the USA. My pastor is now the president of the country of Malawi!

My closing challenge: What God expects is obedience. It is the key to everything in our faith walk. Faith doesn't make things easy; rather, it makes things possible. Whatever you do for God, remember to give Him all the glory. "Cause me to know the way in which I should walk, for I lift up my soul to You." (Psalm 143:86 NKJV)

FORTY-YEAR PRAYER ANSWERED

Sandy

How Great Thou Art

*"O Lord, my God, when I in awesome wonder,
consider all the worlds Thy hands have made…"
(Carl Gustav Boberg, Sweden, 1885)*

The sign at the church reads: "Mom prayed for forty years for someone to come to Jesus, and they did. Never give up praying."

I was sixteen when Mrs. Christie started praying for me. I met her when she came to see my family after Dad died. She was nice, but I told her, "I don't want to receive Jesus as my personal Savior. You can just keep right on praying,"

Mrs. Christie was already in Heaven when I finally surrendered. Her son was on the team at a retreat I attended. He told me that the sign was hanging in his church that's when I realized how God works bringing people into our lives.

I was born in Massachusetts, perfect, except my bones were misaligned, not being formed right in the womb.. Growing up in a small house in Kentucky with my parents and a brother and a sister, I was distressed that the atmosphere of our alcoholic home was constantly filled with arguments and fighting.

Both parents and I spent months in the hospital with tuberculosis; in fact, my father had most of his lungs removed. However, he continued to drink and smoke heavily when he returned home. I recovered from TB, but I had damaged emotions resulting from my chaotic, and sometimes abusive, childhood. However, I was a good student and was active in sports.

After I graduated from high school, I married a man with two children. I found I couldn't count on him, and the marriage ended. For many years I felt lonely and bereft of a meaningful life. There was a deep emptiness. I searched all types of religions, Science-based, Native, and New Age, but I knew none of them held the answers I needed.

One Sunday I went to an evangelical church where I felt the presence of God for the first time. I attended a few more times until one Sunday I opened the door of my heart and invited Jesus to come in and become Lord of my life. I was baptized in the Atlantic Ocean in Florida. I smiled when I thought of Mrs. Christie and how she had promised to pray for me forty years before. I had been spiritually dead, now I was spiritually alive.

Since then, I have relied on Jesus, the only One I can count on. He has never given up on me and always has kept His Word. Through good or bad times His presence has been constant. When I have sought to do His will, He has brought the right people into my life and has orchestrated the right circumstances. I try to be ready to be obedient at all times when He opens a door. Also, I have learned that nothing is too hard for God.

On a personal note, I have accepted the bone deformity becoming convinced that I was created by God. I have been able to relate to people with special needs, the homeless, the sick, and the elderly. You could say the ministry God has given me is practical! "Is this not the fast that I have chosen: to loose the bonds of wickedness, to undo the heavy burdens, to let the oppressed go free…Is it not to share your bread with the hungry? When you see the naked that you cover him?"
(Sections from Isaiah 58:6-7 NKJV))

AMERICA IN MY HEART

Lierte

In Christ Alone

"In Christ alone my hope is found. He is my light, my strength, my song..." (Keith Getty and Stuart Townsend, 2001)

"You're asking me to preach? I'm only ten!" I had jumped to my feet in the pastor's office. I was thrilled but fearful at the same time.

"I already spoke with your mother and father. They both felt you could do a fine job. The LORD will guide you."

I knew it was a great opportunity and agreed to prepare for my first sermon. It was a blessing for me, and the listeners were blessed.

At that time, my Brazilian family was living in America. Even though we returned to Brazil, my love for the USA never left me. I am filled with joy that I am telling my story from the wonderful land of freedom where I became a citizen.

I was born and raised in Governador Valadares with a Brazilian Christian family. My father and mother greatly influenced my young life. We had home Bible studies every day and went to church Sunday evenings, the only time services were held there on Sundays.

When I was a teenager, an evangelist from Louisiana, Bobby Ready, came to Brazil. He asked my parents if they'd give their permission for me to travel with him. "Yes." answered my dad, "The Lord's will be done." I traveled in Brazil with Bobby for ten years participating in city-wide meetings. During that time I studied English. After that, every summer I traveled with American evangelists translating their sermons. I graduated from seminary in Brazil.

America never left my heart; however, I didn't think of living there permanently. I did visit friends and preached there occasionally. Pastor Ready shared that New England needed missionaries. I never forgot his words.

Later, I pastored a church and planted ten churches in the city where I lived, three outside the city, and one in the mountains. The tug to go to America was strong, so I applied for a green card after my wife agreed to go with me and to raise our son in America..

The day before I left, a friend kidnapped me. For twenty-four hours he tried to convince me not to go. Using his attempted persuasion, he pointed out how the ministry had grown, how we had three services, and how we were on television regularly. He couldn't move me no matter how hard he tried.

It wasn't easy to leave Brazil, but, like Abraham, (Genesis 12) God called me to leave everything and to go where He directed. My family is close, and it was heart wrenching to leave all of them. Saying goodbye to the church people was very hard for me as well.

Now I pastor two churches one in Vermont's country setting and one in Massachusetts where there is a bi-lingual, multi-cultural community. When I was a boy in the USA, our team was losing a kickball game. A girl had shouted, "Go back where you belong!" I came back to where I belong, America, now my home as a full-fledged citizen.

You aren't reading this by accident. A dot can change your life forever. God will show you how to connect the dots. Remember, even though you see yourself as weak, God can help you fulfill your purpose. "Trust in the LORD with all your heart, and lean not on your own understanding." (Proverbs 3:5 NKJV)

A LIGHT TO FOLLOW

Janice

Turn Your Eyes Upon Jesus

> *"Turn your eyes upon Jesus; look full in His wonderful face, and the things of earth will grow strangely dim..."(Helen Lemmel, England,1922)*

"Fire! Fire! Come quick!" My twin, Francis, saved my life that day when we were barely five years-old. Incidentally, we were known by most of our community as Jan and Fran.

It all started because I wanted to burn my tricycle so I could get a big girl's bike. I was using a stick poking the fire in our backyard burn barrel. I kept sticking the hot stick onto the trike until the fire caught the sash of my dress. My twin ran in the house to get Dad. He ripped off the burning dress and rolled me on the ground. Then, he took me to the hospital where the doctors told my parents that I had little chance of surviving. I did survive by God's grace.

1/3 of my body sustained third degree burns. I will never forget that month in the hospital and the many surgeries of skin grafts. But that was when I learned the faithfulness of God. My whole life I have known His watchful care and faithfulness.

My twin and I were born in Virginia adding to two older siblings. From birth we went to church, which was central for our family. Every Sunday my large extended family met at my grandparents' home for lunch to eat the scrumptious meal my grandmother had cooked. I was close to my grandfather and learned ethics from him. I'll never forget him giving me advice. "You're only as good as your word. Work hard and take responsibility."

Our family life was chaotic and frightening. My father, a pilot, was unhappy, and he was mean to all of us. We took turns hollering a warning. "He's coming!" He would make us line up similar to the way the Captain in the musical, *Sound of Music*, did. When one of us was naughty, he spanked all his children. My mother divorced him when she realized he wasn't going to change. My pastor and his wife, along with my church family and paternal grandparents helped me heal from the breakup of our family.

After there was a moral issue of the youth leaders and they left, our church and youth group of fifty was destroyed. After that, I went in a wrong direction and began to hang out with "new" friends. One day I met someone who I thought was "the man of my dreams." I married him on my eighteenth birthday. He was handsome with a magnetic personality, but my parents were wary of him. I had idolized that twenty-two year old man from when I was only sixteen.

Life with my husband was a nightmare; he was emotionally and verbally controlling especially when he drank or imbibed drugs. He demanded I ask him to take me places and forbade me to drive myself. My husband was irate when I bought a car for myself.

One day I was so desperate I nailed every window shut, locked the doors, and piled his personal belongings on the porch. Then I left with my toddler, a beautiful little girl who didn't deserve to grow up in a chaotic home. I moved us out-of-state; my husband called and apologized asking me to come back. He insisted that he'd changed.

God always looked out for me. I was married for eleven years trying to "make it work." We separated several times, but God had planned my future. I went to college and graduated with a BA in Business Management specializing in finance while my godly neighbor babysat. I saved so I could get my own apartment. The LORD ordered my steps that broke my dependence on my husband: (1.) Job, (2) Car, (3) Education, (4) Apartment, (5) Baby sitter.

One day I knew I'd had enough of my tumultuous marriage. While my husband was at work, I loaded up half of our belongings and moved into an apartment. We were divorced, and I have never gone back to my home state.

Even though I was baptized at twenty-three, I hadn't fully yielded my life to Christ. My second husband and I met at work; I received Christ as my Savior and Lord of my life after we were married. We recently celebrated our thirty-first anniversary.

My path of life changed from trouble to a good life of serving the lord together in a happy marriage. From the terrible burns to the difficult marriage, I know God was always lighting the way for this Southern Belle. I learned to trust that He would make a way, and He did! "You will keep him [her] in perfect peace, whose mind is stayed on You, because he [she] trusts in You." (Isaiah 26:3 NKJV The author added [].)

WHEN HE BECAME LORD

Lisa

Jesus Paid it All

> "I hear the Savior say, 'Thy strength indeed is small. Child of weakness, watch and pray. Find in Me thine all in all...'" (Elvina Hall, USA, 1865)

"Mom, we need God in this house!" My youngest daughter of three interrupted my frustrated tirade. I'm sure my mouth looked like that of a fish out of water. I ran into my bedroom and told God I was surrendering to Him as the tears poured down my face soaking an area of my bedspread.

That was the beginning. For nine months I struggled as I gradually let go of the worldly lifestyle. I began a journey with the lover of my soul. Love, joy, and peace filled our home more and more after I made the choice to surrender to the lordship of Jesus Christ.

I remember learning that my father was in the pulpit while I was being born. My father read from the Bible that wives must submit to their husbands, and he enforced it. Therefore, my childhood was chaotic, and I think that caused me to feel anxious. My parents fought frequently, so I tried to be a peacemaker between my parents forgetting about my own needs. Later, I prayed they'd split up. When I was fourteen, they did divorce. I went with my father, and my sister went with my mother.

In a deep insecurity, I went away from the LORD during my teen years. I sought the company of "underdogs." Also, I didn't guard myself in my relationships with the boys and men in my life. The Bible warns: *"Guard your heart with all diligence, for out of it flow the issues of life."* (Proverbs 4:23) I married at eighteen and got divorced at twenty.

I graduated from a hairdressing school at nineteen and used that education to support my four children as a single mother for seventeen years. My stable career wasn't enough to bring joy into our home. My youngest daughter knew that God could make the difference. Since I let Him be the Lord of my entire life, Jesus gave back what I thought I had lost and even added more. When He became LORD, I began to know Him as the lover of my soul.

It had been my choice to surrender, and I know that was pivotal for all that has happened since that day. God opened doors so that I could own a hairdressing business. One day I received a call that a salon had become available two minutes from my house. All the equipment was included. I got a business loan and set up shop. The first order of business was to put up a plaque that read: *"The Lord is gracious."* Psalm 145:8.

Now I am married to a kind Christian man who has completed our family. There are six children since I adopted my two granddaughters. I dearly love all the spouses too and my many grandchildren. I thank my LORD every day for His bountiful blessings.

> *"Delight yourself in the Lord, and He will give you the desires of your heart." (Psalm 37:4 ESV)*

BEYOND THE EXPECTED

Barbara

Chain Breaker

"If you've got pain, He's a pain taker.
If you feel lost, He's a way maker...
(Zach Williams, USA, 2016)

My daughter, Sarah, is a gift from God. I was admitted to the hospital because of heavy bleeding. Imagine my shock when the doctor remarked that my baby was fine. "BABY?? I had my tubes tied about ten years ago and had a D&C two months ago! No, you're wrong, doctor; I'm not pregnant!" He ordered an ultrasound to be sure the baby was not in the tubes. Everything was fine.

About a week after being discharged from the hospital, I was driving when I saw Jesus coming toward me with outstretched arms. He was dressed in white with a gold shawl around his neck. *Was I going crazy?* No. From that day He helped me change my life so that I have been sober for over twenty-five years. He gave me a daughter who is truly a gift. Sarah and I have frequent life challenges, but we are together through everything. Only God could have done all this. My hope is that my story will inspire readers to believe God can break their chains!

New York was my birthplace. I ended up being a middle child having two older brothers and a younger sister and brother.

My earliest memories are of spending time with my cousins when we played kickball and other games. I enjoyed going to my aunt's home to watch slides of the family. On Saturdays Dad took all of us to the dairy where he worked. The secretary gave us cream sickles. I hated them. I liked her, though, so I ate them.

Everything changed when I found myself pregnant at sixteen. I was in New York, and the father was a boy I had been seeing for two summers. I gave birth to a son; then I married someone I had crushed on as a teen.

My husband and I lived with my mother-in-law. Unfortunately, they ganged up on me with constant unkindness and physical abuse, which led to a trend. But after I left him and moved back home, I found out I was expecting his child.

I divorced him after a struggle; my angry, red-faced husband shouted "If I can't have you, then nobody will! I will kill you first!" Later, he granted me a divorce but only after he had met a woman he wanted to marry. Coincidentally, she and I have children that were born around the same time, so it became obvious that he had already been cheating.

I married my second husband which was why I wanted a divorce. Otherwise, I wouldn't have cared. We lived in New York moving around the same city because of the landlords who didn't take care of their apartments, otherwise known as slumlords.

After 6 years of marriage, we were also divorced. I met and dated another man; that's when I found out I was pregnant against all odds.

My sense of well-being and identity suffered when I was assaulted sexually by a grown man when I was fourteen. I confided in two family members who both brushed it away. There was a deep pit inside me that I tried to fill with relationships and alcohol. Counselors wanted to help me get over my bad memories, fears, and insecurities. *How could a therapist help me untangle the tight knots of my life*? Only Jesus could do what didn't happen during years of therapy.

Because of Jesus filling my life, I am a new person. He is 100% my LORD and Savior, and I thank him every day for breaking the chains! He is my lifeline.

> *Be true to yourself and to God. Things will turn out better than you ever hoped. "Now faith is the assurance of things hoped for, the conviction of things not seen." (Hebrews 11:1 NIV)*

ALL THINGS MADE NEW

Sonja

Great is Thy faithfulness

*"Great is Thy faithfulness, O God, my father.
There is no shadow of turning with Thee…"
(Thomas Chisholm, USA, 1923)*

Kenny Rogers! That can't really be him! I had gone into the musical theater that my school had rented for my high school graduation, to rehearse the solo I would sing. Apparently, Kenny Rogers had been listening. "You have a very special voice, little lady." He smiled at me.

While in college, I connected with a band and toured with them as the lead singer on weekends. After college, I traveled with the band two weeks out of every month.

Yes, I have won awards and have seen amazing places, but none of that satisfied the deep void in my heart. I found that satisfaction only in my Lord and Savior. He tore down the mess I had made of my life and built it up to fulfill His purpose.

I entered the world in Warwick, Rhode Island with a giggle; the attending nurse exclaimed, "This is a happy one!" My older brother, younger sister and I had a happy childhood. I have cherished many memories of my family being together. Good family memories are more important than things. My parents pointed us in the right direction without causing harm.

A memory is when I was a junior in high school. There was a national public speaking contest called "Voice of Democracy." The judging was in Washington, DC, and I won third place. For a sixteen year- old it was exciting to travel to the capital, all expenses paid. I spoke before congress and President Reagan, who passed me a beautiful box containing a medal.

When I was in third grade I started singing in church. At ten I sang in chapel and in the choir at the Christian school I attended. I loved church music and often sang solos. Singing for the Lord was rewarding, but I wanted to enter the national singing competition. My dream came true when I got that opportunity. I received medals for solo, duet, and trio on that trip.

For the last two years of high school I transferred to a public school. I endured some bullying, but, overall, I enjoyed those years. Then, in college I majored in Interior Design and minored in Architecture. I was happy with my educational studies, but I was itching to sing.

There was a sign posted in a store window: **LOCAL BAND NEEDS A LEAD SINGER.** I auditioned and got the position. The band members went out to drink in bars, and I stayed behind. It was a grueling schedule, classes during the day, band at night and on weekends. There was a disruption when I contracted mono; I quit the band until I was over it. Then, I graduated and resumed singing with the band until choices of music became very dark.

I never kept my relationship with Jesus secret, but I made some relationship choices that were not in my best interest. I was engaged until I found out my fiancé was cheating. In my broken state I sought to find a church. At my new church I was offered the position of worship leader. I dated a man who was on the worship team and left the church when we broke up. Shortly afterward, I became engaged again. My pastor was strongly opposed to the marriage, but I went ahead and married him anyway. Although I tried to make it work, it ended in a divorce. My brother came immediately to live with me when my husband moved out.

After several upsetting church incidents, my feelings of betrayal turned into bitterness then into hatred (toward people, not God). I thought I'd never be a part of a worship team or get married again. I'd made a tangled mess of my life. God had to tear it all apart so He could make the tapestry of my life beautiful the way He intended. "Father, I want you to be #1 in all I do. Help me to heed your voice and to follow your leading. I don't need anything this world has to offer, only Jesus."

Everything became new. I had a first date with my future husband. We connected so well it seemed we had known each other for twenty years. Joy overflows in our marriage as we're serving God and learning to minister together. Yes, I am worship leader at our church. In a few weeks we'll have completed a ministry school associate degree program. I can't birth children, but I love being a stepmom. I have a dream job with weekends off.

> *A reminder to me is: "For what use is it to gain all the wealth and power of this world, with everything it could offer you, at the cost of your own life? And what could be more valuable to you than your own soul?" (Mark 8:36-37 TPT)*

A PARTY BROUGHT HOPE

Paul

I Can Only Imagine

> *"Surrounded by Your glory, what will my heart feel? Will I dance for You, Jesus? Or in awe of You, be still?" (Bart Millard, USA, 2001)*

"Do you want to party like you've never partied before?" My friend waited for my answer.

"Sure. Where is it?" I smiled and bumped Guy's shoulder.

"It's for me to know, and for you to find out. Come on. Hop in."

We pulled into the parking lot of a store front. Lights were on, and through the window I could see people moving around. I followed my friend inside. Imagine my surprise when I realized I was in a Christian coffee house. That is where my whole life changed, and I've been partying with Jesus ever since.

I was born in Boston, Massachusetts, a 2 1/2 month preemie. I weighed 43 ounces at birth but dropped to a mere 18 ounces soon after I was placed in an incubator. Doctors gave my parents little hope of my survival. I fought to live, and two years after my birth, a birth certificate was finally issued!

That was the beginning of a lifetime of survival challenges. When I was three years old, I was diagnosed with cerebral palsy. I'll do my best to explain what it is. The disability is basically a brain injury, a permanent injury. Sadly, that part of the brain will never function. My treatment goal was to coax uninjured parts of my brain to make up for the part that didn't work. Actually, I endured many treatments only because of my mother' singing distraction.

I'm sure my mother had many sleepless nights and bouts of frustration, but she always had a smile and kind words for me. My father was harsh toward me because he wanted to toughen me up. Both parents and my siblings never knew what might be coming up the pike where I was concerned.

When I was seven, both legs were in casts from the hips and a rod from one ankle to the other with my legs as far apart as they would go. I lived in a children's hospital school for five years. I started school at five years old but went back to first grade when I was ten.

As a teenager, I felt useless and hopeless. Suicidal thoughts swirled in my brain. A Christian family, who faithfully lived for the Lord, befriended me. I was strung out when one of the sons invited me to the coffee house. They never treated me like a cripple; they showed me God's love. I had hope and began my journey of independence.

I went to trade school and graduated with honors, one of the top ten of 310 in the class. I found I had an aptitude for mechanics and other hands-on skills. I worked hard and became an automobile mechanic. I cut down trees, milled them, dug a foundation, laid cinder blocks, and built me a house. I had a life!

Totally surrendered to the Lordship of Christ, I was able to overcome a terrible temper. I learned to safely release pent up feelings. I became better at relationships. Sometimes it had taken me two years before I would open up to someone I had such severe social anxiety.

Recently I earned a degree in ministry. Using the mechanical ability, I started "Fix-it for Ministries. A donation of a wheelchair that needed work was fixed and given to an amputee. After I fix something that is donated I sell it with the payment going to a ministry. I fix vehicles and give them away. Smaller machines like lawnmowers and snow blowers get fixed and sold.

>
> *I love helping people find hope like I found. No matter who you have been or what you have done, Jesus loves you, and so do I. "This hope is a strong and trustworthy anchor for our souls…" (Hebrews 6:19a NLT)*

LIGHT FROM DARKNESS

Anne

All creatures of our God and King

*"All creatures of our God and King lift up your
voice with us: Sing. Alleluia! Alleluia!"
(St Francis of Assisi, Italy, 1225)*

"The horse galloped across the finish line." Since I was a girl I have loved animals especially horses; that's why all of the novels I write include some of God's four-legged creatures.

Yes, I write inspirational novels. I spent much of my childhood in boarding schools and only saw my family during Christmas break and in the summer. I was lonely and depressed. My mind was filled with stories, and the characters became my imaginary friends. Deep inside I heard God speak to me. "Rely on me, not the story characters,"

I did learn to rely on the LORD. After ten years, the inner voice told me to write the stories. I answered "No" several times because I loved the characters in my mind that weren't real. "The stories are in your head; I want them to come out into the light." So far, seventeen novels have been published. My name is Anne Perreault; I write inspirational novels about faith, relationship challenges, and redemption. Now my own story is being published. How cool is that!

I was born in Hamburg, Germany during a storm. My father was First Officer; he gave me a boat with a tiny wheel that became my playground when I was about four. I steered my little boat in Stockholm, Sweden with my Pipi Long Stocking doll propped up beside me.

I grew up in Germany, Austria, England, and also Dubai, my vision of Paradise. In America I lived in New England states, New Hampshire, Vermont, and Connecticut. I felt like a bouncy ball. My life was chaotic, and I had fears of abandonment. However, I was close to my grandparents and loved dipping my toes into the frigid ocean water when on our vacations.

My school experiences were so confusing they reminded me of trying to piece together a 3,000-piece puzzle. In the German schools, free-thinking was not allowed. In fact, career paths were set for all the students. German was my first language, and English was my second. The language barrier was significant when I began going to a private British school in Dubai.

Finding my love for horses in Dubai, I learned to ride by persistence after falling more times than I can count. When I became a trainer of Arabian race horses at fourteen years old, I felt I had found my destiny. I taught horseback riding for fifteen years and was a certified therapeutic riding instructor.

I earned a master's degree in secondary education with a major in biology. Once I was with a group of students planning a college trip to Russia when the door opened and a tall, gangly man hopped over to us. *If he was wearing green, he could be a giant frog!* We got acquainted during the trip, and I have been married to this goofy, kind man for thirty-one years, and we have been blessed with three amazing children.

When we were expecting our youngest, our doctor harassed us to get an abortion because he said a test showed Downs. During every appointment, my husband and I told him, "We will not agree to an abortion." That doctor was so wrong: our son was born perfect. We can't imagine what our family would be without him making us laugh. You see, he's a bit "goofy."

When I was a child I felt God's presence, but I was lonely and often depressed. I boarded at an inn in Austria where two teachers lived. One of them took me to a Bible study. However, it took twelve years for me to give my whole life to Jesus. I waited for "the other shoe to drop." Trusting God was hard for me.

I dealt with moments of distrust and fear while thinking of stories. I loved the characters I created. A story became my hiding place, and the characters became my friends. God whispered to my spirit, "Rely on Me, not the story characters." I focused on prayer and heard the directive, "Write the story, Daughter."

"No, I love the people who aren't real."

"The story is in your head, but I want it to come out into the light."

At a ladies' retreat I finally became obedient to the heavenly calling I had resisted for ten years. *I am called to be an author.* I lacked confidence in a big way; then, I began to understand my Heavenly Father's love. "I know how much you love the characters. You are real flesh and blood. I love you."

> *Light from darkness—distrust and fear was replaced by a desire to bless others. I have written forty+ stories and seventeen have been published, all written to encourage the readers. I know for certain that inspiration comes from above. OH, YES! There's no doubt… "Behold, I will do a new thing. Now it shall spring forth. Shall you not know it?" (Isaiah 43:19a NKJV)*

HEAVENLY RESCUE

Teresa

Because He Lives

"Because He lives, I can face tomorrow. Because He lives, all fear is gone…And life is worth the living just because He lives." (Bill and Gloria Gaither, USA, 1971)

"We have come to take care of you." I was in my friend's car and was waiting for the overdose of pills to take effect. My brain swirled with tormenting thoughts of regret. If it felt good, I had engaged in it, booze, drugs, and promiscuous activities, all to gain a peace of mind. I had damaged emotions of feeling unacceptable and unloved.

The woman peered at me and smiled. "Come on. You're not okay. Get in our car." I got in the backseat beside a boy, and she got in the passenger seat.

A man looked at me in the rearview mirror and smiled. "You'll need to rest and eat." We drove a short distance and parked in the driveway of a small house. The front door was unlocked, and we entered the living room. The woman showed me to a bedroom, helped me onto the bed, and slipped off my shoes. "Rest here now. I'll make some food for you."

I rested and ate some spaghetti. Afterward, I felt lighter, and my mind was clearer. They brought me back to my friend's car. I thanked them, and the man said, "Our work here is done."

The pills I had taken had absolutely no effect. I later looked for the house and the helpful people but to no avail. Though I wasn't walking with Jesus at that time, I knew in my heart that He had sent angels to care for me. From that day, my outlook on life was changed.

I was born in France on Thanksgiving Day. My mother called me her little turkey. My father was in the Army; he was a strict parent. We lived mostly in the mid-west during my childhood.

When I was around eight years old, my parents made me babysit my three younger brothers, and when I was ten, it was my responsibility to cook our dinner and wash the dishes. I was shy so I found it difficult to make friends. At night I was plagued with nightmares.

One Easter I received a little chick. Henny-Penny became my friend following me everywhere. I was happiest when I played with my very own pet hen. Even now, I miss my Henny-Penny.

I received salvation when I was seven at Vacation Bible School. I was always close to an aunt who loved me, never judging my actions or decisions. She was the first person who interested me in the person of Jesus. I regularly attended church, but I continued to experience mental torment and oppression. Billy Graham's television broadcasts caused me to understand more about God's purpose for my life.

As I progressed into my teens, I wanted to be accepted. Therefore, to be accepted I engaged in wild and dangerous activities.. *Where could I find peace?* I enlisted in the Army and became a Nuclear Weapons Specialist learning to assemble bombs. My fellow soldier became my husband, who I married forty years ago. We have a daughter, son-in-law, and two grandchildren, a delightful boy and beautiful girl.

Realizing the implications of my heavenly rescue from a suicide attempt, I rededicated my life to the LORD. Although I had walked away from Him, He was always calling me back. I know now that He never left me even for a moment. I could have died several times, but He rescued me and showed me how to live in peace. Also, He set me free from the unwanted and tormenting thoughts.

I found that there were only two ways to live. One was to pursue worldly pleasures in an effort to gain satisfaction. Satan tried to lure me to his way that would have brought destruction of my soul. The other path was the way of life for now and in eternity. I made the choice for that way, to receive Jesus, who has satisfied me with a fulfilling life.

> *"The thief comes only to steal and kill and destroy;*
> *I (Jesus) am come that they may have life,*
> *and have it to the full." (John **10:10** NIV*
> *() author's insert)*

FROM FEAR TO FAITH
Carol

Gentle Shepherd

*"Gentle shepherd come and lead us,
for we need you to help us find our way…"
(Gloria Gaither, USA, 2003)*

"Your doctor prayed by your side every day." Those were the first words I heard after being unconscious for nine days. At eighteen years old, my body was shutting down. Many health issues had ravaged my body because of my "party" lifestyle.

While in the hospital, I committed my whole life to Jesus. He filled my lonely heart with love and peace. The story of my life is one of survival from rejection and abandonment as well as abuse by several people.

I found the Good Shepherd who would always make a way and guide me through "the valley of the shadow of death." I learned that He is always making a way; all I have to do is follow. He convinced me that He will never love me more when I've done better nor love me less when I've done worse.

I was born in Bangor, Maine and only weighed three lbs. at birth since my mother smoked and drank throughout her pregnancy. My parents had lived in Germany, but the military had sent them to the United States.

My earliest memory is the sound of fighting. My father left us not even saying goodbye to us. I stayed with Mom until I was taken from her due to neglect. At five I was on the street while she frequented bars. I remember riding my bike until two in the morning at that age.

A neighbor lady, Mrs. Lapp, brought me and my bicycle to her house. I fell asleep quickly from exhaustion. She brought me to her church on Sundays. Actually, I was with her in her house more often than I was at home with my mother and whoever she was entertaining on any given night. Believe me when I tell you, I saw things no little child should ever see.

Mrs. Lapp decided to intervene and eventually found my father. There followed a custody hearing, and he was court-ordered to have full custody while my mother was determined to be unfit to raise me. Oh, was my father ever angry about the ruling! He complained, "I never wanted you." Since the divorce he had remarried and had a stepson. Every day he and his wife were unloving and excessively strict toward me; they were not the same toward my step brother. In fact, he was given all my toys.

There was a bright spot, though, in my dreary life, my paternal grandmother. She was a godly woman who conveyed a positive and spiritual influence. I always knew she loved me, especially when she made my favorite cookie, soft molasses. An edict came down that I was not to ever have any sweets. It was all very secret, and I hid to eat them. Seeing her as an example of a follower of Christ, I wanted what I witnessed in her consistent life. I committed my whole self to my LORD picturing a circle with me in the middle. I gave Jesus everything in the circle. I was going to need my gentle shepherd to lead and protect me every minute of every day.

When I turned eighteen, I left and went to live with my mother. There was alcohol, drugs, and regular partying. I soon fell into an unhealthy lifestyle. That's when I ended up dying in the ICU. My body was shutting down from malnourishment and a rare case of mono. My mother and my inebriated step father came to see me, and the hospital staff insisted that they leave. Then, my father got called, but he didn't come. I felt I had no one who cared.

The social worker found a lady who agreed to care for me until I recovered. I stayed with her and recovered fully. During that time, I rededicated my life to the Lord determining to follow His lead.

Securing a nice apartment and managing a store, I had a good life. I met my husband on a Naval Base where he worked. We married, but it wasn't "happily ever after." It wasn't long before I discovered his true self, the day he punched me in the stomach. I had some reprieve every time he left for six months for his work in the Navy.

As time passed, he was caught having an affair. I was scared to confront him. We had three kids, and he threatened to take them away from me. My mother-in-law wasn't supportive; in fact, she snatched them as newborns and kept me from them for a week. I had no support from her. She and her son were both "control freaks." I did know I had support from my grandmother, my doctor, and Mrs. Lapp.

Three times my children and I fled to battered women's shelters. When I returned home, my husband was more controlling. In order to get groceries I had to take money from his wallet while he slept. He had rages when he trashed the house or assaulted one of us. I was filled with fear and had panic attacks. He would shout, "If you leave again, I'll take the kids."

I remember how Satan wanted me to succumb to depression and suicide. Because of the nagging fear, I couldn't just walk out. It had to be in God's timing. I surrendered to the care and leading of the Good Shepherd and finally left my husband.

Our leaving came about when a lady called, "Your husband's gun is ready." I didn't know about the gun so I approached my husband. "Why sneak the gun?"

He replied, "You don't want to know." Violence led to the sheriff coming to our house and I told him all that had gone on. From his place of employment the police led him to jail in handcuffs. They found guns in his car. God rescued the children and me; I had stopped my own efforts and had prayed that the LORD would deal with all of it. Whenever I had tried to change the circumstances myself, everything would fall apart. Only He had the plan of success.

"I am the good shepherd; the good shepherd giveth His life for the sheep... My sheep hear my voice, and I know them, and they follow me."
(John 10:14, 27 KJV)

ALL FOR HIS GLORY

Doreen

I Surrender All

*"All to Jesus I surrender; all to Him I freely give.
I surrender all; I surrender all…"*
(Judson W. DeVenter, USA, 1896)

"We have to get her to the OR stat!" I was an obstetrics nurse, and I knew I was called upon…to pray for my patient who had given birth moments before and now was hemorrhaging. I held her baby boy who was perfect at 8 lbs. 4 oz.; he stared into my eyes while I prayed for his Mama. I prayed for this little one too as I looked at his long dark lashes and his slicked-back brown hair. I whispered, "God has your mama in His hands."

I heard someone come into the room. I turned and came face-to-face with the husband. His whole body was trembling. "Nurs-s-e, I-I can't lose my-y wife."

I was trembling too and sent up a quick prayer. "She's in good hands. Rest assured that they know how to help her. God has His hand upon your wife. May I pray with you?"

Yes, please." We prayed, and the father and mother brought their baby home in just two days.

When I was in nursing school, I declared that I never wanted to be an OB nurse. However, I've spent my career years as one.

Determined that my work would glorify God in all I said and did, I know I have failed with that many times. JESUS HAS NEVER FAILED ME!

I was born in Springfield, Massachusetts in 1952 the baby of my family with an older brother and sister. My parents moved us so many times I had difficulty in making childhood close friends. However, I had a good family life.

I wasn't quite eight when I was admitted to the hospital for a short stay. The nurses were attentive to my every need besides being always kind and compassionate. *I want to be a nurse when I grow up!* When I returned home I set up a first aid station on our porch.

I did follow my childhood dream and went to a residential nursing school. After graduating with my RN license, the only nursing job I was able to get was in, you guessed it, obstetrics. It was in New Mexico among the Native Americans. One situation stands out; a husband shot his pregnant wife. Thankfully, she survived giving birth to a healthy girl. That mother was so thankful for her care she named her daughter, Doreen, after me. Another incident was when a chanting medicine man hovered by the hospital bed of a severely ill patient attempting to bring her back to health. There were emergencies and deliveries, and I never knew what to expect.

One day I was thrilled to see that one of my classmates had joined the nursing staff. When we talked, she excitedly shared her born- again experience explaining changes in her attitudes and life styles. I became interested as she planted seeds of truth during our many conversations. She explained how Jesus was the Lamb of God, sinless and born of a virgin. I asked lots of questions that she patiently answered. "He came to be the substitute taking your punishment by His death on the cross. He loves you that much."

I thought my life was spinning out of control when my longtime boyfriend called," I've made plans to move to Alaska."

Only God could help me get through that loss. "I give my life to you. Come in by your loving Holy Spirit. I have made a mess of my life, so please take control. Forgive me! Help me!" Peace came over me like I'd never felt before. In the meantime, my brother had become born again too.

I searched for a church and decided to attend with a small congregation the next Sunday. Once a team from a Bible college came there, and I knew I was being led to attend. There was a student who took an interest in me. I liked his personality and sense of humor a lot; we married and completed one year of study. Recently, we celebrated our forty-fifth anniversary.

The Lord's fingerprints were all over my life. I loved to sing in choirs and play the accordion, and I was blessed to go on mission trips where I used my nursing skills. Also, there were many opportunities to share from the Bible.

A great trial centered on the birth of our dear baby girl. Alysa Marie lived only six days. Early tests had shown she would have serious birth defects, and we were counseled to abort her. I carried her full term. My heart was filled with love as I held my sweet baby to my chest and then released her into the arms of my Savior who loved her more than I did.

There is a section of scripture that is a comfort to everyone who has a little one in Heaven. The newborn son of King David lived for seven days. Afterward, his servants questioned his eating food and going on with his life. His answer states, "But now he is dead; why should I fast? Can I bring him back again? I shall go to him, but he shall not return to me." (II Samuel 12:23) We were blessed with two biological children, a girl and boy, and two girls for whom we had legal custody until adulthood.

During my career in obstetrics, Jesus' presence has been with me through all I have experienced, such as a uterus turning wrong side out, stillborn babies, and mothers and babies not making it out of the delivery rooms. One time I went to a morgue to get a baby to bring to its distraught mother. I leaned on the Lord during every hour of every day. He kept me alert to opportunities to pray and to speak words of comfort. Most of the time, I shared in the joy of healthy births.

> *The verse that has guided my life is: "And whatever you do, do it heartily, as to the Lord and not to men." (Colossians 3:23 NKJV)*

BUT FOR GRACE

Jenny

My Defender

"Though I walk through the valley of the shadow…I will know that I'm not forsaken…"
(Jeremy Camp, USA, 2017)

Decisions! Decisions! Decisions! I made some that put me in monumental danger, and I know some humungous angels protected me. I started taking drugs when I was just a nine year-old girl and continued sporadically throughout my young adult years. One time I, a white girl, was on the street in Harlem waiting for my junkie boyfriend. It was a dangerous situation to be sure, but I was unharmed.

Many times I hitchhiked being picked up or dropped off even in filthy areas sometimes. Another girl and I were back packing and hitchhiking when we hitched a ride with a man who didn't want to let us out. We managed to jump out when he slowed for a traffic light.

There were other times when I know God was protecting me, like the time a woman pointed a gun straight at me. I escaped that fate because of God's intervention. A boldness came over me, and I deescalated the situation.

My story centers, though, on the decisions that led me on a path of grace, mercy, joy and peace. Now, I always inquire of the Lord before making any decisions.

I was born in the Bronx, New York, the only girl with two older brothers. Although I was close to my father and grandmother, I disliked my environment and other family members, especially my mother. There were inappropriate sexual advances and activities and also pornography in my neighborhood. My family left the Bronx, but I hated the life I was forced to live after we moved to Queens, New York. This young New Yorker was miserable and turned to drugs and a wild life.

Although I wasn't encouraged to participate in extra-curricular activities, I enjoyed gymnastics and high diving. In my teen years I worked in hospitals and stables.

When I was seventeen, I saw a poster in a breakroom where I worked at a hospital during my senior year in high school. ***Let your Light so shine before men, that they will see your good works and glorify your Father in Heaven.*** **(Matthew 5:16-18)**. I read that and wondered where I could discover the Light. It wasn't long before I met a Christian girl at a friend's house. *Where did she get such happiness?* She shone her light in my direction while she answered my questions and gave me *The Good News Bible*.

I read, "For it is by God's grace that you have been saved through faith. It is not the result of your own efforts, but God's gift, so that no one can boast about it." (Ephesians 2:8-9) My heart responded causing tears to flow. I knew I didn't deserve God's grace, but it was a gift that He was holding out to me. I received the gift of salvation and have lived for God ever since that day I made the decision.

I "did it my way," but after I was saved I "did it God's way." For instance, I told my boyfriend that there would be no more sleeping together. We broke up when he didn't want to respect my choice.

Jesus became the answer to all my questions. My "dark" choices had brought more darkness, and now my "light" choices bring more light. I am filled with joy and peace, and I pray every day that I will let my light shine to those around me.

> *"God you are my righteousness, my Champion Defender. Answer me when I cry for help...I need your kindness right away! Grant me your grace, hear my prayer, and set me free!" (Psalm 4:1 TPT)*

Part Two
Author's Responses to the Stories

CHAPTER ONE
Training Children

*"Train up a child in the way he should go,
and when he is old, he will not depart from it."
Proverbs 22:6 (KJV)*

To train a child is to give them an appropriate start in life while teaching them to differentiate between right and wrong. The motive must be love as we read in I Peter 4:8, "Most important of all, continue to show deep love…" (NLT) God's love in and through us (agape), is a nurturing attitude toward children that will help bring them to maturity.

Sadly, several of the stories in this book reveal the opposite. Parents may scream at their children. "I hate you! I want to kill you! I wish you were never born! You're dumb! You're stupid! You'll never amount to anything! I'll break you like a horse!" I've known children who suffered at the hands of those who abused them regularly, verbally, sexually, and physically. When confronted, a parent may respond, "I was just disciplining him/her." Yet, the child may have been too frightened to even act naughty for discipline to even be warranted.

This chapter will explain why I believe strongly that children are valuable human beings who have the right to a safe, happy, and peaceful young life. My discussion here centers on the issue of spanking. Spanking is usually defined as the use of physical force with the intention of causing a child to experience pain, but not injury. Spanking is a common event in homes across America, and it is legal in many states for it to be administered in schools. Although the main purpose is often the attempt to control behavior, I have come to a personal conclusion that frequent spanking is inappropriate punishment because it brings about harmful effects. However, I do realize there are those moments when a spanking is the only effective measure to change some dangerous or inappropriate behavior, especially blatant rebellion.

The first harmful effect is that children who experience spankings may become confused. What causes this confusion? Parents and teachers tell children not to hit, but then those adults hit them. Children learn by example and role models. Some people who believe in spanking quote the Bible; "Spare the rod and spoil the child." The verse actually reads: "He who spares his rod hates his son, but he who loves him disciplines him promptly." Proverbs 13:24, NKJV. Nowhere does Scripture say parents should administer punishment by hitting their children with sticks. The rod, a shepherd's equipment, was always used to guide sheep, never to hit them.

Some people believe spankings are effective for teaching children about consequences of their behavior in the same way that adults see jail or fines as a consequence of theirs. Confusion may be caused from being hit for no reason except that an authority figure becomes angry for some reason that may not even involve the child. I feel that confusion can often come because the child has no idea why they are being struck resulting in stress and anxiety and may cause lifelong problems. Ephesians 6:1-4 states: "Children, obey your parents in the Lord, for this is right. Honor your father and mother, which is the first commandment with promise *that it may be well with you and you may live long on the earth*. And you, fathers, do not provoke your children to wrath…" NKJV

Another effect of spanking is that it causes resentment toward parents and teachers. Spankings may leave a child resentful of authority. Hostility may be suppressed for a long time in someone's mind and emotions. Angry feelings may come from being spanked too hard for a minor infraction, and older children are always spanked with more force. Poor relationships with authority figures may affect all future relationships as the person struggles with inner rage.

I don't agree with some advocates that spankings make children feel more loved when they are told, "I am showing you I love you by this spanking." This is not a good example of what love feels like. I know this hostility does not always occur; some people do beat the odds and become kind and loving. The vast majority, however, will carry violence over to the next generation.

Another effect of corporal punishment is that children who are spanked tend to engage in anti-social behavior and substance abuse. I think this is from the stress which violence causes. From volunteer work I have done in correction facilities, I have discovered that violence produces violence. I have talked with several prisoners who are full of rage because of parental abuse.

In conclusion, I believe that children should have the right to protection. Corporal punishment is not the only way to eliminate undesirable behavior. Another way is simply not to reinforce it by using alternatives that may work better. Sometimes giving information, demonstrating right behavior, giving choices, and changing the environment may be helpful to alter undesirable behavior, especially for young children.

In conclusion, I don't think that violence does much to change a child's behavior; instead, it often causes confusion, hostility, and more violence. **It has been said that the line between acceptable punishment and abuse is easily blurred!**

CHAPTER TWO

Inspiring Youth

Teens are seeking attention, love, and acceptance. If only we'd spend time listening to them, we could help them navigate the rough waters of adolescence, including depression, anxiety, and panic attacks. Following are some of my observations and methods for effective ministry to the twenty-first century teens.

The media often provides an introduction to violence and immorality perpetrating the following messages: "If it feels good, then, do it! Right or wrong is what you feel. Truth is what you choose to believe is truth. Live and let live. Look out for #1." In the twenty-first century culture, there are often no boundaries that help kids feel safe and secure. Wanting to "Be cool!" teens have cell phones, ipads, computers, and televisions that they habitually operate in their bedrooms late at night. Cell phones are constantly in use. Many parents make no plans for monitoring usage. In fact, parental influence is sorely missing in the lives of many of today's teens.

Some people think that adolescents in the twenty-first century are the same as always, declaring, "Kids have always been kids. Things may change on the surface, but teenagers have always been with us and have always pushed the extremes of adult society. They are basically the same now as they were thousands of years ago. Only the styles have changed." Others say that those behaviors have become more frequent and have gotten increasingly worse.[1]

Twenty-first century teenagers deal with many issues unheard of when I was their age. They are confronted with school closings due to bomb threats, school shootings, social networks, increased bullying, and parental problems. Contemporary teens have less support than teens had fifty years ago when most of them had extended families nearby.

Social networks, texting, music, online games, DVDs, television, movies, school, and books are now influencing today's teen culture. Their attitudes, values, behaviors, and identities are being shaped. For instance, teens are overly "body conscious." They may wear revealing clothing and view sexuality only as lust. Their "idols" may be inappropriate role models, and they can travel anywhere in the world via phones or computers.

In the Bible, the term *world* refers to these environmental factors. *The world, the flesh, and the Devil* all contribute to human suffering. The "world" represents outer forces that may bring about crises. The "flesh" includes a lack of judgment, poor decisions, and the giving in to the dictates and desires of the body and mind. I believe The Devil tirelessly tempts, flatters, and deceives teenagers.

Leaders in the teen's spiritual community must not push and cajole; these young people have tender souls. Some are angry with God, and some even question His eternal existence. Also, observing what they see as hypocrisy may turn them off to all spiritual discussions. Jesus was kind, but firm, in His dealings with people, and his people should try to follow His example. Lamentations 2:18b-19 says "Give yourself no relief; give your eyes no rest. Arise, cry out in the night, at the beginning of the watches; pour out your heart like water before the face of the

---

[1] Chap Clark and Steve Rabey. *When Kids Hurt: Help for Adults Navigating the Adolescent Maze (*Grand Rapids,,MI: Baker Books, 2009). 17

Lord. Lift your hands toward Him for the life of your young children, who faint from hunger at the head of every street." NKJV Prayer will be effective as we pray for our young people often.

CHAPTER THREE

Supporting Women

"I tried to think of ways to get her to counseling, ways to help her. Then I realized I couldn't make that decision for her. She had to make it herself…I will mourn and pray for her, but I will not lose hope. I rejoice that He makes beauty from ashes, and I am excited about how He is taking me to a deeper level of faith and trust in Him." As we relate to this resolve of a friend to help by praying, we may think that is all we can do when we recognize problems a friend may be experiencing within her marriage.[1]

I want to discuss women's issues from the premise that there are effective principles that can be learned and followed. After being confronted with domestic violence issues revealed by wives, some spiritual leaders have taken the husband's side or have called in a dangerous husband for a couple's counseling session Following either of those two situations, the violence may escalate when the man becomes angry because private things of their home had been revealed by his wife.

It is imperative that we help women find freedom, safety, and support. Every desperate cry for help should be heard and taken seriously. My hope is that women and their families will experience freedom from life-controlling problems through effective ministry. Here are some goals:

---

[1] Moore, Beth. *Breaking Free: The Journey, The Stories* (Nashville, TN: Life Way Press, 2009) 126

1. *That they will learn to trust in Jesus as their Savior and Lord.* Trust may be a difficult concept for some, so I learned not to be pushy. The Lord will direct every conversation. Proverbs 3: 5,6
2. *That they will want to be free of old thought patterns and behaviors.* This freedom originates from knowledge and choice. The women will learn to be open before the Lord and to make appropriate daily choices. Psalm 139:3.
3. *That they will believe that their lives can be transformed.* Many of these women have believed for a long time that there is no hope for change. Isaiah 43: 2,3a
4. *That they will have a desire to learn from the Word of God.* Some women may have never even seen a Bible. Psalm 119: 101-103

Isaiah 26:3 states, "You will keep him in perfect peace, whose mind is stayed on You, because he trusts in You." It's one thing to develop a steadfast mind; it's another to fight for one's freedom. Many women live their lives in a subjective manner according to their thoughts and feelings at any given moment. Trying to change by depending on personal strength often is ineffective.

Some challenges to overcoming may be unhealthy attitudes such as:

- I am worthless.
- I am a victim.
- I can do nothing about it.
- I am always at fault.
- I am the only one who has had these experiences.

Strongholds in her mind may be those preceding unhealthy attitudes. II Cor.10: 3-5 declares, "For though we walk in the flesh, we do not war according to the flesh. For the weapons of our warfare are not carnal but mighty in God for pulling down strongholds, casting down arguments and every high thing that exalts itself against the knowledge of God, bringing every thought into captivity to the obedience of Christ." NKJV

In Romans 12: 2 the Apostle Paul explains that we are "transformed by the renewing of our minds." I have always referred to the concept as *unlearning* and *relearning*. The last part of Philippians 4: 8 states, "…whatever things are true, whatever things are noble, whatever things are just, whatever things are pure, whatever things are lovely, whatever things are of good report …meditate on these things." NKJV

Only the agape love ("God's love in and through us)," I Corinthians 13:1 Amplified Bible) will be able to break through the walls many women have built up around their hearts. One soul is worth the investment of our time. Jesus said, "For what will it profit a man if he gains the whole world, and loses his own soul?" (Mark 8: 36 NKJV) In Jesus' entire ministry here on this earth, He always showed that His interest was in the individual.

The Holy Spirit has a major role as God's people seek to help others. I seek to leave room for supernatural intervention and often explain that Jesus wants to help the hurting, betrayed woman take steps toward wholeness. Offer to pray, but be sensitive to her response. If she is not ready for prayer, smile and continue the conversation. Never try to force a prayer!

From experience, I know that it is a long process for a woman to move from self- loathing to self- esteem. Patience is needed to build a relationship and to nurture those seedlings of self- esteem. I try to remember that each woman is a unique individual who will always relate to others and the world in her own way. Remember, prayer is powerful!

CHAPTER FOUR
Understanding the New Age

The New Age Movement is not really *new*; it is as old as the Garden of Eden where Satan made an appeal to Adam and Eve that they could be as gods. The media may give the impression that it is *new* and may often focus on its practices to the overlooking of its philosophies and religious leanings.

"Universal energy" replaces the reality of a personal God with the idea that humanity is the center of all things. Many aspects of the New Age are taken from Eastern mysticism, but the religion is not the same as Hinduism or Buddhism. The beliefs in reincarnation and karma are kept, but the New Age has two distinct expressions.

1. Occult practice: crystal power, channeling, and spirit guides
2. Humanism: the development of all human potential leading to godhood.

The goal of the movement is the formation of a utopian society, or A New World Order. People who have a quest for "self-deification" believe they will find "personal enlightenment of the divine within." They engage in "humanistic psychology, medieval witchcraft, and pagan pantheism."

The New Age creed consists of six principles:

(1.) Pantheism: "All is one; therefore, all is god." The New Age gods and goddesses are seen to actually be impersonal beings. God is "universal energy and the oneness of all living things. This energy is in all things." This is a core belief of Hinduism.

(2.) "Humanity, like all creation, is divine and has unlimited potential." People may create their own realities. Humans have no limitations as they visualize and create. They have no absolutes and no accountability but to themselves.

(3.) "Humanity's basic flaw is its ignorance of divinity and oneness with all things." They don't believe the problem is sin, but rather they believe the barrier to further evolution is ignorance of humanity's divinity. The "Awakening" process is called "Transformation."

(4.) "Humanity's only need is transformation—the awareness of divinity." Humans are their own creators and are responsible for everything that happens to them and around them. The "evolutionary process" will produce a sudden appearance of a "fully formed, highly evolved new species."

(5.) "Transformation can be produced by a wide variety of techniques." These will induce an altered state of consciousness. The hope is that a person's current beliefs will be replaced by a new perception of reality. "Almost anything is acceptable that will trigger a mystic or psychic experience powerful enough to cause a person to reject his or her former beliefs and perception of reality."

(6.) "Personal transformation is the springboard to global transformation." To them global transformation means "mass enlightenment and global unity," one monetary system, world government, and world religion. Some believe this includes "one language" and others believe "all people will think the same thought at the same time."

"When feeling a need for spiritual enlightenment, however, the individual must ask, 'If I pursue a New Age teaching or technique, will I find myself dancing in the light or walking in the darkness?'"[1]

IDENTIFYING CULTS

- Opposing critical thinking and isolating dissenters
- Threatening those who want to leave and penalizing those who do leave
- Emphasizing bizarre beliefs and denouncing Scripture and religion
- Leading with demands of inappropriate loyalties
- Dishonoring members' family ties
- Engaging in abnormal sexual practices
- Taking ownership of other's personal property

---

[1] Lochaas, Philip H. *The New Age Movement: How to Respond.* (St. Louis, MO: Concordia, 2010) pages 7-13

www.ingramcontent.com/pod-product-compliance
Lightning Source LLC
LaVergne TN
LVHW020431080526
838202LV00055B/5125